STUDENT WORKBOOK
AVIATION MAINTENANCE TECHNICIAN HANDBOOK

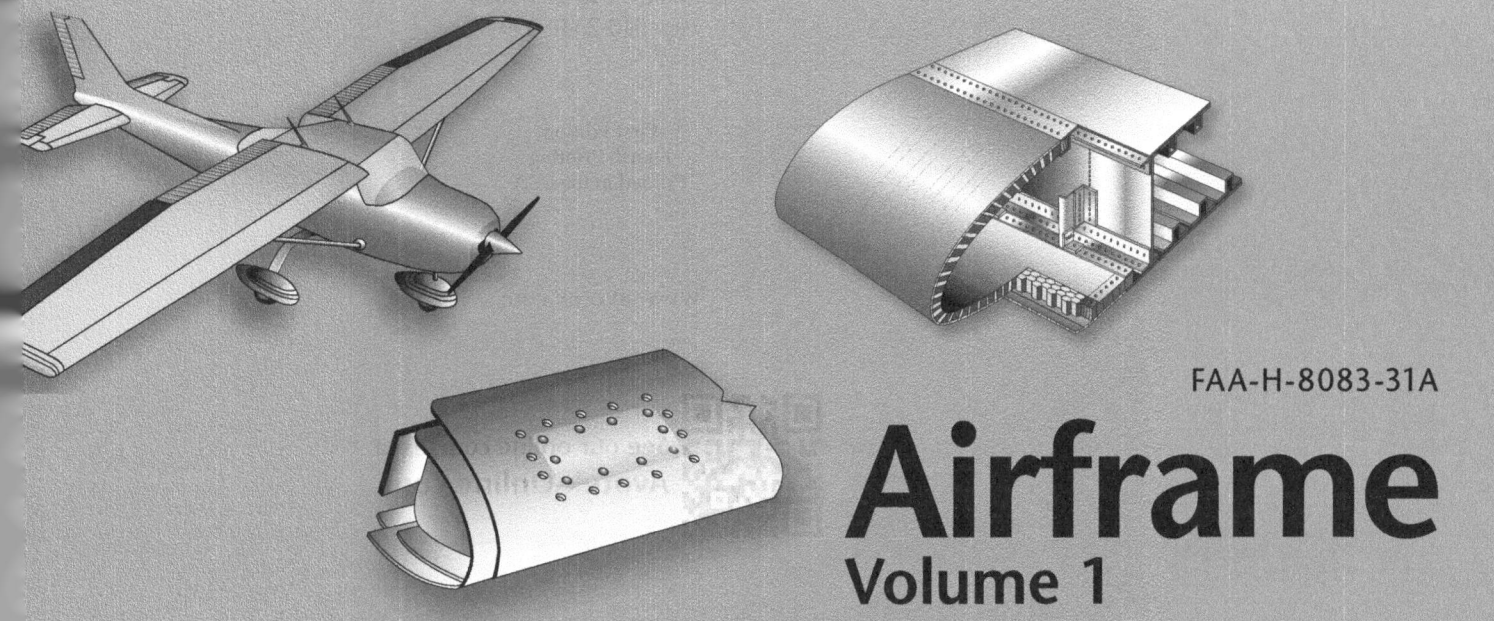

FAA-H-8083-31A

Airframe
Volume 1

Production Staff

Designer/Photographer Dustin Blyer
Senior Designer/Production Manager Roberta Byerly
Contributor David Jones
Editor Jeff Strong

© Copyright 2019 by
Avotek Information Resources, LLC.
All Rights Reserved

International Standard Book Number 1-933189-65-7
ISBN 13: 978-1-933189-65-9
Order # T-FAA-H-8083-31A-AIR-Vol1-0102

For Sale by: Avotek
A Select Aerospace Industries, Inc. company

Mail to:
P.O. Box 219
Weyers Cave, Virginia 24486
USA

Ship to:
200 Packaging Drive
Weyers Cave, Virginia 24486
USA

Toll Free: 800-828-6835
Telephone: 540-234-9090
Fax: 540-234-9399

First Edition
Fourth Printing
Printed in the USA

www.avotek.com

See our online courses at
Avotek-Online.com.

Contents

To the Student — iv

1. Aircraft Structures — 1
2. Aerodynamics, Aircraft Assembly and Rigging — 7
3. Aircraft Fabric Covering — 19
4. Aircraft Metal Structural Repair — 25
5. Aircraft Welding — 37
6. Aircraft Wood and Structural Repair — 43
7. Advanced Composite Materials — 49
8. Aircraft Painting and Finishing — 57
9. Aircraft Electrical System — 63

To the Student

This Student Workbook accompanies *Aviation Maintenance Technician Handbook–Airframe Vol.1*, the second in a three-book series. This workbook should be used as a tool for highlighting the strengths and pinpointing the weaknesses of the AMT student gathering the skill and knowledge necessary to build a strong foundation in the aircraft maintenance field. Specifically, it helps you evaluate the progress made in applicable subject areas.

In writing this workbook, Avotek used the principle that the student is actively engaged in preparing for two goals: the first is to pass all required testing for the FAA Airframe and Powerplant Mechanic Certificate, and the second is to obtain the necessary skills and knowledge to function as an entry-level mechanic in the field. Both goals must be kept in mind and the material presented here has been designed to maintain that balance.

Each chapter of the workbook is divided into three question formats and printed on perforated sheets for removal and presentation. The formats are as follows:

Fill in the Blank
These questions are designed to help the student understand new terminology and fundamental facts essential to the understanding of section material.

Multiple Choice
These questions offer a broader overview of the material by offering several possible answers, and allowing the student to identify the correct answer either through recognition or through the process of elimination.

Analysis
These are complex questions that require the student to access information presented in the text, analyze the data, and record a response. Successful completion of the analysis questions shows the student has a thorough understanding of the material in the chapter.

The answers for each set of questions are available from your course instructor.

Avotek® Aircraft Maintenance Series
Introduction to Aircraft Maintenance
Aircraft Structural Maintenance
Aircraft System Maintenance
Aircraft Powerplant Maintenance

Avionics Series
Avionics: Fundamentals of Aircraft Electronics
Avionics: Beyond the AET
Avionics: Instruments and Auxiliary Systems
Avionics: Systems and Troubleshooting

Other Books by Avotek
Advanced Composites
Aircraft Corrosion Control Guide

Aircraft Hydraulics
Aircraft Structural Technician
Aircraft Turbine Engines
Aircraft Wiring and Electrical Installation
AMT Reference Handbook
Aviation Mechanic Instructor's Handbook
Avotek Aeronautical Dictionary
Fundamentals of Modern Aviation
Helicopter Maintenance
Introduction to Aircraft Structures, Systems, and Powerplants
Light Sport Aircraft Inspection Procedures
Structural Composites: Advanced Composites in Aviation
Transport Category Aircraft Systems

Chapter 1
Aircraft Structures

FILL IN THE BLANK QUESTIONS

name:

date:

1. The first successful powered airplane was built and flown by the Wright brothers in the year _____.

2. The term _____ has come to describe a new generation of jet aircraft made almost entirely of advanced composite materials.

3. _____ is a material's internal resistance, or counterforce, that opposes deformation, whereas the degree of deformation of a material is known as _____.

4. _____ is the stress that resists the force tending to cause one layer of a material to slide over an adjacent layer—for example, in the case of two riveted plates in tension.

5. A/An _____ is usually constructed of steel tubing welded together such that all members can carry both tension and compression loads, and it is usually covered with fabric.

6. The _____ relies largely on the strength of the skin or covering to carry the primary loads.

7. _____ extend across several frame members and help the skin support bending loads.

8. The angle between the horizontal plane of the fuselage and the wing is called the _____.

9. In a/an _____ wing design, the wings have no external bracing but are supported internally by structural members assisted by the skin of the aircraft.

10. _____ are the structural crosspieces that combine with spars and stringers to make up the framework of the wing.

11. _____ are streamlined enclosures used primarily to house the engine and its components, but some are designed to house the retracted landing gear.

12. Some people call it the tail section, but the proper term is the _____.

13. To rotate the aircraft around its longitudinal axis, the pilot uses the _____—control surfaces attached to the trailing edge of both wings.

14. The rudder is the primary control surface that causes an aircraft to _____.

Chapter 1
Aircraft Structures

FILL IN THE BLANK QUESTIONS

name:

date:

15. The _____ are lowered to increase the camber of the wings and provide greater lift and control at slow speeds, shortening the amount of runway required for takeoff and landing.

16. Several types of _____ are used to help a pilot move and hold a control surface during high-speed flight, when the force of air can make it difficult to move the surface.

17. A/An _____ is a vertical upturn of the wing's tip and is designed to reduce the drag caused by wing-tip vortices in flight.

18. _____ does not retract for flight and is used only on simple aircraft that fly at relatively slow speeds.

19. The most common landing gear configuration today is _____, in which a nose wheel is at the forward end of the fuselage.

20. The manufacturer's maintenance instructions supersede the general procedures found in Advisory Circular _____ and _____.

21. All maintenance related actions on an aircraft or component are required to be documented by the performing technician in the aircraft or component _____.

22. The _____ is an imaginary vertical plane at or near the nose of the aircraft from which all fore and aft distances are measured.

23. _____ is the measurement of height in inches perpendicular from a horizontal plane usually located at the ground, cabin floor, or some other easily referenced location.

24. The upper surface of the wings typically have fewer _____ than the lower surface because a smooth surface promotes better laminar airflow.

25. In helicopters with semirigid or fully articulated rotor systems, blades flap up and down due to _____ the relative windspeed is greater on an advancing blade than on a retreating blade.

Chapter 1
Aircraft Structures

MULTIPLE CHOICE QUESTIONS

name:

date:

1. The first tri-wing glider to fly a human was developed by:
   a. Otto Lilienthal in 1896
   b. George Cayley in 1853
   c. Louis Bleriot in 1909
   d. Orville and Wilbur Wright in 1903

2. The first mono-wing aircraft was developed by:
   a. Otto Lilienthal in 1896
   b. George Cayley in 1853
   c. Louis Bleriot in 1909
   d. Orville and Wilbur Wright in 1903

3. Turbine engines and advancements in pressurized cabins were developed:
   a. During World War I
   b. In the 1930s
   c. After World War II
   d. Only in recent years

4. This type of stress resists a crushing force that would otherwise shorten or squeeze aircraft parts.
   a. Tension
   b. Compression
   c. Torsion
   d. Shear

5. Bending stress is a combination of these two stresses:
   a. Compression and torsion
   b. Shear and tension
   c. Shear and torsion
   d. Compression and tension

6. These structural members, used in semimonocoque fuselages, usually extend across several frame members and help the skin support primary bending loads.
   a. Longerons
   b. Stringers
   c. Ribs
   d. Formers

7. The most common material from which wings are constructed is:
   a. Wood
   b. Magnesium alloy
   c. Aluminum
   d. Carbon fiber

8. These wing structural members run parallel to the lateral axis of the aircraft, carry the loads caused by wing bending, and may be solid, box-shaped, partly hollow, or in the form of an I-beam.
   a. Ribs
   b. Bulkheads
   c. Spars
   d. Trusses

9. A "wet wing" means that:
   a. The wing includes deicing systems
   b. Fuel is carried inside the wing
   c. The wing is treated with chemicals to cut wing resistance
   d. The wing is covered with honeycomb structured wing panels

10. These detachable panels cover areas to which regular access is required, such as the engine and its accessories, while also providing a smooth airflow over the nacelle.
    a. Engine mounts
    b. Cowling
    c. Cowl flaps
    d. Pods

11. The primary flight control surface located at the aft edge of the horizontal stabilizer is:
    a. The elevator
    b. The rudder
    c. The flaps
    d. The ailerons

12. The primary flight control surface located on the outboard trailing edge of each wing is counted as part of the wing's surface area and known as:
    a. The elevator
    b. The rudder
    c. The flaps
    d. The ailerons

Chapter 1
Aircraft Structures

MULTIPLE CHOICE QUESTIONS

name:

date:

13. Some airplanes have a control surface called a "ruddervator," which controls the plane's movements around which axes?
    a. Vertical and lateral
    b. Vertical and longitudinal
    c. Longitudinal and lateral
    d. Lateral and posterior

14. Which of these auxiliary flight control surfaces is located on the outer leading edge of the wing and lowers the stall speed by directing wind over the wing when the angle of attack is high?
    a. Balance tabs
    b. Slats
    c. Spoilers
    d. Slots

15. Which of these auxiliary flight control surfaces on the trailing edge of a primary flight control surface reduces the force necessary to move the primary control surface?
    a. Flaps
    b. Spoilers
    c. Balance tabs
    d. Slots

16. This type of tab allows a pilot to take his or her hands and feet off of the controls and have the aircraft remain in its stable flight condition.
    a. Balance tab
    b. Servo tab
    c. Spring tab
    d. Trim tab

17. Spring tabs are one method by which to move a control surface in its final stages of travel; another method, used to assist the movement of ailerons on large aircraft using controlled airflow in and out of the hinge area, is:
    a. A servo tab
    b. A balance panel
    c. A hydraulic actuator
    d. A vent gap

18. A stall fence—a chordwise barrier on the upper surface of the wing that halts the spanwise flow of air during low-speed flight—is most common on:
    a. Wings with a tapered leading edge
    b. Swept wings
    c. Delta wings
    d. Straight-edge wings

19. This part of a helicopter rotor enables changes to the blade pitch angle.
    a. Teetering hinge
    b. EBF
    c. Feathering hinge
    d. Coning hinge

20. Which of these counters the force that tries to spin the fuselage in the opposite direction of the main helicopter rotors?
    a. Tail rotor
    b. Antitorque rotor
    c. Elastomeric bearings
    d. Either A or B

Chapter 1
Aircraft Structures

ANALYSIS QUESTIONS

name:

date:

1. What is the main limitation on monocoque fuselage construction that is solved by a semimonocoque fuselage?

2. What is pressurization and how does it affect the fuselage structure?

3. What materials are used to fabricate wing skin on an aircraft?

4. An aircraft moves around three different axes—longitudinal, lateral, and vertical. For each axis, name one primary control surface and one auxiliary control surface that affects movement around that axis.

Chapter 1
Aircraft Structures

ANALYSIS QUESTIONS

name:

date:

5. What are the advantages of tail wheel landing gear? What are the disadvantages?

Chapter 2
Aerodynamics, Aircraft Assembly and Rigging

FILL IN THE BLANK QUESTIONS

name:

date:

1. Aerodynamics is the study of the dynamics of _____, including the interaction between a moving object and the atmosphere.

2. _____ is usually defined as the force exerted against the earth's surface by the weight of the air above that surface.

3. A column of air, 1 inch square, extending from sea level to the top of the atmosphere weighs approximately _____ pounds.

4. Density varies directly with _____, and inversely with _____.

5. _____ can be caused by the movement of air, the movement of an object through it, or both.

6. Under Newton's first law of motion, air can be considered a "body" because it has _____, and so when it is at rest, it does not move unless a force is applied to it.

7. According to Bernoulli's principle, when air flowing through a tube reaches a constriction, the speed of the air is _____ and the pressure is _____.

8. In the most efficient airfoils, the maximum thickness is located about _____ of the way back from the leading edge of the wing.

9. The _____ of a wing section is an imaginary line that passes through the section from the leading edge to the trailing edge.

10. _____ is the force of gravity acting downward on everything that goes into the aircraft, including the aircraft itself, crew, fuel, and cargo.

11. Lift is to weight as _____ is to drag.

12. _____ is affected by the elevators, the rear portion of the horizontal tail assembly.

13. _____ is the characteristic of an aircraft that tends to cause it to fly (hands off) in a straight-and-level flightpath.

14. _____ can be used to correct any tendency of the aircraft to move toward an undesirable flight attitude by enabling the pilot to correct any unbalanced condition that may exist during flight without exerting any pressure on the primary controls.

15. Flaps, slats, and slots are designed to _____ lift.

Chapter 2
Aerodynamics, Aircraft Assembly and Rigging

FILL IN THE BLANK QUESTIONS

name:

date:

16. _____ is the ratio of the speed of the aircraft to the local speed of sound.

17. In a/an _____ rotor, each blade can move in three directions: rotate about the pitch axis to change lift; back and forth in the rotation plane, leading and lagging; and flapping up and down.

18. _____ occurs approximately 90° in the direction of rotation from the point where the force is applied.

19. For a helicopter to hover, sum of the lift and _____ forces must equal the sum of the weight and _____ forces.

20. The _____, or the law of conservation of angular momentum, states that the value of angular momentum of a rotating body does not change unless an external force is applied.

21. Increasing the _____ of the rotor blades while keeping their rotation speed constant generates additional lift and the helicopter ascends.

22. As airspeed increases, the rotor system completely outruns the recirculation of old vortices and begins to work in relatively undisturbed air, meaning that induced flow and induced drag are reduced—a process known as _____.

23. _____, the state of flight in which the main rotor system is being turned by the action of air moving up through the rotor rather than by engine power, allows a helicopter to land safely if the engine fails.

24. The purpose of _____ is to bring the tips of all blades into the same tip path throughout their entire cycle of rotation.

25. In a reciprocating engine, as the cylinder moves back toward the cylinder head, the fuel/air mixture is compressed; and when compression is nearly complete, the _____ fire and the compressed mixture is ignited to begin the power stroke.

26. If the engine rpm of a helicopter is 2,500, a/an _____ reduction is required to turn the rotor at 500 rpm.

27. Because of the greater _____ of a helicopter rotor in relation to the power of the engine, as compared to the weight of a propeller and the power in an airplane, the _____ must be disconnected from the engine when the starter is engaged through the use of a clutch.

Chapter 2
Aerodynamics, Aircraft Assembly and Rigging

FILL IN THE BLANK QUESTIONS

name:

date:

28. When a control surface is mounted on a balance stand, a downward travel of the trailing edge below the horizontal position indicates _____, usually indicated with a _____ sign.

29. The _____ is a formal description of an aircraft, engine, or propeller issued by the FAA when the FAA determines that the product meets the applicable requirements for certification under 14 CFR.

30. A 7x19 cable consists of seven _____ of nineteen _____ each.

31. Fairleads should never deflect the alignment of a cable more than _____ from a straight line.

32. Before you check the structural alignment of the main components of an aircraft, the aircraft must be jacked and _____.

33. To determine the amount of tension on a cable, use a/an _____.

34. The _____ of a control surface or flight deck control means the prescribed arc through which it must be capable of moving.

35. Protractors are used to measure _____ in degrees.

36. A safety wire should have _____ to _____ twists per inch of wire and be pulled taut while being installed.

37. The two primary conditions that must be met for an aircraft to be considered airworthy are that the aircraft must conform to its _____ and that the aircraft must be in a condition for safe operation.

38. _____ are issued by the FAA when an unsafe condition exists in an aircraft, aircraft engine, propeller, or appliance, and the condition is likely to exist or develop in other products of the same type design.

39. A certificated mechanic with an Airframe and Powerplant (A&P) rating must hold an _____ to perform an annual inspection.

40. Any person operating an airplane in controlled airspace under instrument flight rules (IFR) must have had, within the preceding _____, each static pressure system, altimeter instrument, and automatic pressure altitude reporting system tested and inspected and found to comply with 14 CFR part 43, Appendix E.

Chapter 2
Aerodynamics, Aircraft Assembly and Rigging

MULTIPLE CHOICE QUESTIONS

name:

date:

1. At sea level, the average barometric pressure is:
   a. 14.7 "Hg or 1,000 mb
   b. 29.92 "Hg or 1,103.25 mb
   c. 29.92 "Hg or 1,013.25 mb
   d. 29.25 "Hg or 1,013.92 mb

2. Which of these statements about the density of air is *not* true?
   a. Density varies inversely with the temperature.
   b. Air at low altitudes is more dense than air at high altitudes.
   c. The same amount of air is more dense when it is hot than when it is cool.
   d. The same amount of air is more dense when it is under greater pressure than when it is under lower pressure.

3. The amount of moisture in the air divided by the amount of moisture in the air at the same temperature and under the same pressure could hold is better known as:
   a. Relative humidity
   b. Absolute humidity
   c. Sea-level humidity ratio
   d. Vapor pressure

4. What is the proper term to describe this information: "an aircraft is flying due west at 210 mph"?
   a. Direction
   b. Vector
   c. Velocity
   d. Speed

5. "Force equals mass times acceleration" is the mathematical statement of:
   a. Newton's first law
   b. Newton's second law
   c. Newton's third law
   d. Newton's fourth law

6. Any part of an aircraft that converts air resistance to lift is:
   a. A camber
   b. A venturi
   c. A wing
   d. An airfoil

7. The ratio of a wing's chord to its maximum thickness is called:
   a. The lift-to-drag ratio
   b. The fineness ratio
   c. The angle of attack
   d. The aspect ratio

8. High-lift wings have a:
   a. Large positive camber on the upper surface and a slightly negative camber on the lower
   b. Slightly positive camber on the upper surface and a slightly negative camber on the lower
   c. Positive camber on both the upper and lower surfaces
   d. Negative camber on both the upper and lower surfaces

9. The angle between the chord of an airfoil and the relative wind is called:
   a. The angle of incidence
   b. The angle of attack
   c. The stall angle
   d. The thrust angle

10. To maintain steady, horizontal flight, which two forces must be equal?
    a. Lift and drag
    b. Thrust and drag
    c. Lift and weight
    d. Thrust and weight

11. If an aircraft at equilibrium is disturbed by, for example, a gust of wind and the amplitude of the resulting motion decreases over time, the aircraft is said to possess:
    a. Dynamic stability
    b. Longitudinal stability
    c. Static stability
    d. Lateral stability

12. The tendency of an aircraft to return to its original attitude following a rolling motion is called:
    a. Dynamic stability
    b. Longitudinal stability
    c. Static stability
    d. Lateral stability

Chapter 2
Aerodynamics, Aircraft Assembly and Rigging

MULTIPLE CHOICE QUESTIONS

name:

date:

13. A control system that employs electrical signals to transmit the pilot's actions through a computer to various flight control actuators in known as:
    a. Hydromechanical control system
    b. Mechanical control system
    c. Fly-by-wire control system
    d. IVR control system

14. The greatest drag on flight is experienced:
    a. At subsonic speeds
    b. At supersonic speeds
    c. At intersonic speeds
    d. At transonic speeds

15. The tail rotor on a helicopter compensates for: The torque generated by the main rotor
    a. The shear forces generated by the main rotor
    b. Wind resistance
    c. The drag produced by the main rotor

16. The angle of attack of rotor blades increases when the pilot increases their:
    a. Speed
    b. Pitch
    c. Lift
    d. Tip-path plane

17. To ascend vertically, a helicopter must generate:
    a. More lift and drag than thrust and weight
    b. More thrust and drag than lift and weight
    c. More lift and thrust than weight and drag
    d. More weight and drag than lift and thrust

18. This helicopter control is used to make changes to the angle of attack of all main rotors.
    a. Antitorque pedals
    b. Collective pitch control
    c. Throttle control
    d. Cyclic pitch control

19. This helicopter control allows the pilot to fly the helicopter in any horizontal direction.
    a. Antitorque pedals
    b. Collective pitch control
    c. Throttle control
    d. Cyclic pitch control

20. When a control surface is mounted on a balance stand, a downward travel of the trailing edge below the horizontal position indicates:
    a. Underbalance
    b. Overbalance
    c. Static balance
    d. Dynamic balance

21. If 2 lbs. of material 10 inches behind the balancing point is removed from an airfoil, how much weight must be added to the airfoil 5 inches forward of the balancing point?
    a. 1 lb.
    b. 2 lbs.
    c. 4 lbs.
    d. 5 lbs.

22. Areas where cables pass through battery compartments, lavatories, and wheel wells are prime sites for:
    a. Distortion
    b. Corrosion
    c. Fatigue
    d. Wire strand breakage

23. This is a mechanical screw device consisting of two threaded terminals and a threaded barrel, used for making minor adjustments in cable length and for adjusting cable tension.
    a. Solid fairlead
    b. Turnbuckle
    c. Tension regulator
    d. Pushrods

24. Measurements taken from a given point on either side of the top of the tail fin to a given point on the left and right horizontal stabilizers are used to check for fin:
    a. Rigidity
    b. Incidence
    c. Verticality
    d. Asymmetry

25. Measurements taken with a steel tape and a spring scale between, for example, the wheel well and the front of each wing-mounted engine, or between the wing tips and the front of the tail fin, are used to check for:
    a. Rigidity
    b. Incidence
    c. Verticality
    d. Asymmetry

26. When performing an aircraft conformity inspection, start with this document.
    a. Airworthiness Directive
    b. Type Certificate Data Sheet
    c. Service Bulletin
    d. Pilot's Operating Handbook

27. This type of inspection program is an alternative to annual inspections.
    a. 100-hour inspection
    b. Manufacturer's inspection program
    c. Powerplant inspection
    d. Progressive inspection

28. According to 14 CFR Part 43.15, each person performing a 100-hour or annual inspection must use this when performing the inspection:
    a. Electronic testing equipment
    b. A checklist
    c. An engine stand
    d. An equally qualified partner

29. A commuter aircraft with nine or fewer seats can be inspected under an owner-developed and FAA-approved AAIP, or:
    a. Approved Annual Inspection Program
    b. Annual Aircraft Inspection Project
    c. Approved Aircraft Inspection Program
    d. Administrative Aircraft Inspection Proposal

30. Inspection requirements for aircraft that hold more than 20 passengers are codified in:
    a. 14 CFR Part 121
    b. 14 CFR Part 125
    c. 14 CFR Part 135
    d. 14 CFR Part 119

Chapter 2
Aerodynamics, Aircraft Assembly and Rigging

MULTIPLE CHOICE QUESTIONS

name:

date:

Chapter 2
Aerodynamics, Aircraft Assembly and Rigging

ANALYSIS QUESTIONS

name:

date:

1. How does atmospheric pressure influence the density of air?

2. State each of Newton's three laws of motion and give an example or illustration of each.

3. Describe how an airfoil acts in accordance with Bernoulli's principle. How much of an aircraft's lift is generated by this?

Chapter 2
Aerodynamics, Aircraft Assembly and Rigging

ANALYSIS QUESTIONS

name:

date:

4. Explain the difference between a wing's angle of incidence and its angle of attack.

5. Describe several types of drag and explain what contributes to them, and what can be done to reduce them.

6. What is ground effect and what effect does it have on helicopter operation?

Chapter 2
Aerodynamics, Aircraft Assembly and Rigging

ANALYSIS QUESTIONS

name:

date:

7. What part of a helicopter transmits control inputs from the collective and cyclic controls to the main rotor blades? How does it work?

8. Describe how a turbine engine on a helicopter works.

Chapter 2
Aerodynamics, Aircraft Assembly and Rigging

ANALYSIS QUESTIONS

name:

date:

9. Define aircraft rigging. What specifications describe the rigging of a given aircraft?

10. Describe how rigging and structural alignment are checked during inspection. What angles or measurements are usually checked?

Chapter 3
Aircraft Fabric Covering

FILL IN THE BLANK QUESTIONS

name:

date:

1. The primary advantage of using fabric to cover an aircraft is that fabric is _____.

2. _____ fabrics such as cotton and linen last only five to ten years on an aircraft that sees regular use.

3. In the 1950s, the introduction of _____ fabric as an aircraft covering solved the problem of the limited lifespan of other coverings.

4. An approved _____, usually held by the seller of aircraft covering materials, allows a shop to re-cover an aircraft with materials and processes other than those with which it was originally certificated.

5. A/An _____ is a minimum performance standard issued by the FAA for specified materials, parts, processes, and appliances used on civil aircraft.

6. _____, which is the first coat applied to polyester fabric after it is attached to the airframe and heat shrunk, surrounds the fibers in the fabric with a protective coating to provide adhesion and keep out dirt and moisture.

7. Fabric is considered to be airworthy until it deteriorates to a breaking strength less than _____ of the strength of the new fabric required for the aircraft.

8. In the _____ method of re-covering, multiple flat sections of fabric are trimmed and attached to the airframe.

9. Sharp edges, metal seams, the heads of rivets, and other features on the aircraft structure that might cut or wear through the fabric should be covered with _____ before the new fabric is applied.

10. Most covering procedures for polyester fabric rely on _____ or _____ seams as opposed to _____ seams.

11. The amount polyester fabric shrinks is directly related to the temperature applied; it can shrink nearly _____ at 250 °F and _____ at 350 °F.

12. Usually, _____ uses a single length of cord that passes completely through the wing from the upper surface to the lower surface, thereby attaching the top and bottom skin to the rib simultaneously.

13. Typically, _____ are located at the lowest part of each area of the structure—for example, the bottom of the fuselage, bottom of the wings, or at the bottom of the trailing edge of each rib bay.

Chapter 3
Aircraft Fabric Covering

FILL IN THE BLANK QUESTIONS

name:

date:

14. _____ made from the same polyester material as the covering fabric are applied to all seams, edges, and over the ribs to protect these areas by providing smooth aerodynamic resistance to abrasion.

15. Applied after the sealer coats, the fill coats contain aluminum solids that block _____ from reaching the fabric, thereby increasing its lifespan.

Chapter 3
Aircraft Fabric Covering

MULTIPLE CHOICE QUESTIONS

name:

date:

1. Nitrate dope protects fabric and adheres to it well, but its main drawback is its:
   a. Inability to tauten fabric over the airframe
   b. Flammability
   c. Limited durability
   d. Lack of UV protection

2. The number of threads per inch in a fabric's warp or filling is known as:
   a. The count
   b. The ply
   c. The bias
   d. The greige

3. An edge of cloth that is woven to prevent raveling is called a:
   a. Pinked edge
   b. Greige edge
   c. Selvage edge
   d. Bias edge

4. Which of these is *not* a legal means by which an aircraft can be re-covered with a material other than its original covering material?
   a. Perform the work in accordance with an approved Supplemental Type Certificate
   b. Obtain one-time approval from the FAA Flight Standards District Office
   c. Perform the work in accordance with a Technical Standard Order
   d. Do the work in accordance with a Type Certificate Data Sheet for the new process, secured by the manufacturer

5. This material holds ribs in their proper place and alignment during the covering process.
   a. Reinforcing tape
   b. Rib bracing tape
   c. Rib lacing cord
   d. Martin clip

6. Which of these covering systems uses a water-borne base and EkoFill as a filler and UV block?
   a. Air-Tech
   b. Ceconite/Randolph System
   c. Stits/PolyFiber
   d. Stewart System

7. In preparing the airframe for re-covering, the leading edge of the wing is a critical area because:
   a. The fabric covering will be much thicker than in other areas.
   b. A smooth, regular surface is crucial because airflow diverges there and begins its laminar flow over the wing.
   c. In most cases, the wing structural members are replaced at the same time the aircraft is re-covered.
   d. The usual varnish or primer used on other areas of the aircraft cannot be used there.

8. Which of these methods is recommended when using an iron for heat shrinking a fabric covering?
   a. Start with a high temperature setting and work down to a lower setting for final shrinkage
   b. Move the iron slowly in a straight line from one end of the work to the other, then repeat on a parallel path
   c. Begin heat shrinking when the sealer coat is still damp to the touch
   d. Start at one end, then move to the opposite end, and switch from side to side before finishing the shrinking in the middle of the surface

9. Unless otherwise noted in the manufacturer's instructions, the maximum spacing of rib lacing in the prop wash area of an aircraft with a V_{NE} of 150 mph is:
   a. 1 inch
   b. 1.5 inches
   c. 2.5 inches
   d. 3.5 inches

Chapter 3
Aircraft Fabric Covering

MULTIPLE CHOICE QUESTIONS

name:

date:

10. The widest finishing tape is usually used:
    a. Closest to the propeller
    b. Rib lacing areas
    c. Wing tips and empennage surface edges
    d. Wing leading edges

Chapter 3
Aircraft Fabric Covering

ANALYSIS QUESTIONS

name:

date:

1. How can you determine fabric strength when inspecting an aircraft? What nondestructive methods are available?

2. Describe some of the safety procedures you should observe during the re-covering process.

3. What is the purpose of the sealer coat? How is it applied?

Chapter 4
Aircraft Metal Structural Repair

FILL IN THE BLANK QUESTIONS

name:

date:

1. Aircraft metal structural repair is complicated by the requirement that an aircraft be as _____ as possible.

2. The thickness of sheet metal is designated by a/an _____ number, with the higher numbers denoting _____ metals.

3. Cold forming of aluminum is usually done at _____ temperature.

4. Calculations involving tension must take into account the member's _____, meaning the gross area minus the metal removed by drilling holes or other changes.

5. If a rivet subjected to shear stress gives way, the riveted parts are _____.

6. A/an _____ is a pointed instrument used to mark or score metal to show where it is to be cut, but these marks should be made only when they will be removed by drilling or cutting.

7. The _____, which because of its size is used in a fixed location in the shop, provides a convenient means of cutting and squaring sheet metal via a stationary lower blade attached to a bed and a movable upper blade attached to a crosshead.

8. Aviation snips have colored handles that indicate the direction that the tool cuts— _____ handles mean the tool cuts straight; _____ means the cut curves left; and _____ means the cut curves right.

9. The recommended drill speed for a 1/4-inch drill bit through aluminum, where the recommended sfm is 200, is _____ rpm.

10. _____ drill bits are designed for hard materials like titanium.

11. _____ is the process of toughening steel by gradually heating it and cooling it; it also makes it softer and easier to form.

12. Any bend formed on a bar folder can also be made on the _____ or the _____, because the metal can pass through the jaws in any length without obstruction.

13. The _____ is a machine used to form sheets of metal into cylinders or other straight curved surfaces.

14. To temporarily hold sheet metal parts in place, you can use reusable _____ for lighter parts or _____ fasteners when greater clamp-up pressure is needed.

Chapter 4
Aircraft Metal Structural Repair

FILL IN THE BLANK QUESTIONS

name:

date:

15. Since aluminum alloys do not possess the corrosion resistance of pure aluminum, they are usually treated with a protective cladding such as _____.

16. Aluminum designated by the number _____ is used where strength is not crucial, in areas such as fuel tanks, cowlings, and oil tanks.

17. The _____ rivet is the most common type of rivet used in aircraft construction.

18. Rivets have a/an _____ head on one end, and at the other end, the installation process forms a second head called a/an _____.

19. Rivets with a/an _____ head are used where flushness is required and aerodynamic smoothness of the surface is critical.

20. For a rivet designated with the code MS 20-426-AD-3-8, the diameter of the shaft is _____.

21. If the thickness of the skin material is 0.075 inch, the rivet diameter selection should be _____.

22. The recommended edge distance when using 1/4-inch diameter rivets is about _____.

23. Rivet _____ is the distance between the centers of neighboring rivets in the same row; it should never be less than three rivet diameters, and it is usually four to six rivet diameters.

24. The standard countersink has a/an _____ angle to match the most common countersunk rivet head.

25. If the rivet diameter is 3/16 inch, the final hole should be drilled with a _____ drill bit.

26. _____ is the process of making an indentation around a rivet hole to make the top of the head of a countersunk rivet flush with the surface of the metal.

27. If the shank of an installed rivet buckles, you must replace the rivet with one that is the proper _____.

28. When removing a rivet, work on the _____ head and start by filing a flat area on that head.

29. The _____ process thins, elongates, and curves sheet metal.

Chapter 4
Aircraft Metal Structural Repair

FILL IN THE BLANK QUESTIONS

name:

date:

30. _____ is folding, pleating, or corrugating a piece of sheet metal in a way that shortens it or turning down a flange on a seam—for example, to make one end of a piece of pipe slightly smaller so that it may be slipped into another section.

31. The _____ is the curved section within the bend, or the portion of metal that is curved in bending.

32. In a 90° bend, the _____ equals the radius plus the thickness of the metal.

33. The total developed width of a piece of metal with one or more bends will always be _____ than the total of the mold line dimensions.

34. To find the total developed width using a/an _____, first place a straightedge connecting the bend radius on the top scale to the material thickness on the bottom scale.

35. When bending a box, it is necessary to remove material to make room for the intersecting bend radii, and this is usually done by drilling or punching _____ at the intersection of the inside bend tangent lines.

36. Contact between _____ and magnesium, aluminum, or cadmium can result in corrosion of those metals.

37. _____ is a type of nickel-chromium-iron super alloy typically used in high-temperature applications, including in aircraft powerplant structures.

38. _____ is the lightest structural metal in the world, but it can be difficult to form at room temperature.

39. Although it is 30 percent stronger than steel and 50 percent lighter, _____ and its alloys are mainly used in aircraft parts that require good corrosion resistance, moderate strength up to 600 °F, and light weight.

40. _____ rivets to standard close-tolerance steel fasteners should be used when installing titanium parts.

41. A joint is critical in _____ if more than the optimum number of fasteners are installed; the material may crack and tear between holes, or fastener holes may distort and stretch while the fasteners remain intact.

42. A/An _____ rivet is one that has movement under structural stress, but has not loosened to the extent that movement can be observed, but can sometimes be indicated by a dark, greasy residue or deterioration of paint and primers around rivet heads.

Chapter 4
Aircraft Metal Structural Repair

FILL IN THE BLANK QUESTIONS

name:

date:

43. FAA Form _____, Major Repairs and Alterations, must be completed for repairs to box beams, wings, wing stringers and chords, spars, and other critical parts when the repair involves strengthening, reinforcing, splicing, or replacement.

44. The _____ patch is an external patch, used in areas where aerodynamic smoothness is not important, where the edges of the patch and the skin overlap each other and the overlapping portion of the patch is riveted to the skin.

45. If the damage to a stringer exceeds _____ of the width of one leg and is less than _____ inches long, the stringer must be repaired by cutting out the damaged area, inserting a filler, and attaching a single reinforcement section to the inside of the stringer and to the filler.

Chapter 4
Aircraft Metal Structural Repair

MULTIPLE CHOICE QUESTIONS

name:

date:

1. Which of these statements about stress across a repair is *not* true?
   a. A repair must accept the stresses on the part and carry them across the repair.
   b. Stresses are divided at a repair—they act up to the repair, and then separately on the other side of the repair.
   c. The cross-sectional area across a repair should be consistent.
   d. Stresses flow through the structure, so there should be a continuous path for them.

2. The stress that resists a force that tends to pull apart is called:
   a. Torsion
   b. Compression
   c. Tension
   d. Bearing

3. Which of these is a combination of two stresses?
   a. Torsion
   b. Compression
   c. Tension
   d. Bearing

4. This layout tool consists of a steel scale with three heads that can be moved along the scale and locked in place.
   a. Rivet spacer
   b. Divider
   c. Combination square
   d. Scribe

5. This tool is used to make indentations in metal as an aid in drilling accurate holes.
   a. Center punch
   b. Transfer punch
   c. Scribe
   d. Prick punch

6. Since the head of this saw can be turned at any angle, it is useful for removing damaged sections of a stringer.
   a. Circular saw
   b. Nibbler
   c. Squaring shear
   d. Kett saw

7. The tapered end of a file that fits into the handle is called:
   a. The tang
   b. The face
   c. The teeth
   d. The holder

8. A file with a small number of large teeth is a:
   a. Bastard file
   b. Single-cut file
   c. Coarse file
   d. Dead smooth file

9. Out of these choices, which is the most accurate tool for drilling a hole in sheet metal?
   a. Pneumatic drill
   b. Drill press
   c. Extension drill
   d. 45° drill

10. Out of these choices, which type of drill bit would be the likely choice for drilling a new hole in aluminum?
    a. A single-fluted cobalt alloy drill bit
    b. A three-fluted cobalt alloy drill bit
    c. A double-fluted high-speed steel drill bit
    d. A four-fluted high-speed steel drill bit

11. Which of these drill bits makes the largest hole?
    a. Size 60
    b. Size A
    c. Size 1
    d. Size S

12. This tool is used to enlarge holes and to finish them smooth.
    a. Reamer
    b. Drill bushing
    c. Hole burrer
    d. Chip chaser

Chapter 4
Aircraft Metal Structural Repair

MULTIPLE CHOICE QUESTIONS

name:

date:

13. Which of these brakes can handle the thickest metal sheets?
    a. Cornice brake
    b. Press brake
    c. Box and pan brake
    d. Finger brake

14. This machine, used to form curves in sheet metal, has three solid cylinders. The first two cylinders feed and grip the metal, while the third gives the proper curvature to the work.
    a. Slip roll former
    b. English wheel
    c. Hydropress
    d. Spin former

15. Which of these aluminum alloys is most commonly used in propeller blades?
    a. Alloy 2017
    b. Alloy 2025
    c. Allow 5052
    d. Alloy 5056

16. Which of these aluminum alloys can be used for making rivets and in applications where aluminum comes into contact with magnesium alloys?
    a. Alloy 2017
    b. Alloy 2025
    c. Allow 5052
    d. Alloy 5056

17. Which of these aluminum alloys is weldable?
    a. Alloy 3003
    b. Alloy 2017
    c. Alloy 6061
    d. Alloy 2024

18. Which of these rivets cannot be installed in the condition in which they are received, but must first be annealed?
    a. AD rivets
    b. DD rivets
    c. E-type rivets
    d. Both AD and DD rivets

19. If an AD rivet with a diameter of 1/4 inch is to be installed in material with a total thickness of 3/8 inch, what length rivet should be used?
    a. 1/2 inch
    b. 5/8 inch
    c. 3/4 inch
    d. 7/8 inch

20. What is the minimum spacing between two flush head rivets with a diameter of 1/4 inch?
    a. 1/2 inch
    b. 1 inch
    c. 1 1/2 inches
    d. 2 inches

21. This type of rivet cannot be used in fluid-tight areas, in engine intake areas where rivet parts could enter the engine, or on aircraft control surfaces.
    a. Solid-shank rivets
    b. Double flush rivets
    c. Blind rivets
    d. Annealed rivets

22. The center of this type of rivet can sometimes fall out due to vibration, and this greatly reduces its shear strength.
    a. Friction-lock blind rivets
    b. Mechanical-lock blind rivets
    c. Stem-lock blind rivets
    d. DD rivets

23. Which of these does *not* require a technician to be able to access both sides of the fastener in order to install it?
    a. High-shear fastener
    b. Pull-type lockbolt
    c. CherryMAX bulbed rivet
    d. Both B and C

24. This fastener, which provides a threaded hole in its center, is used to install fairings and trim that must be installed after an assembly is complete.
    a. Rivet nut
    b. Pop rivet
    c. Blind bolt
    d. Lockbolt

Chapter 4
Aircraft Metal Structural Repair

MULTIPLE CHOICE QUESTIONS

name:

date:

25. Among all the aircraft metals, this one is the most easily formed.
    a. Stainless steel
    b. Magnesium
    c. Aluminum
    d. Titanium

26. The line at which the metal in a formed bend starts to curve is called the:
    a. Mold line
    b. Setback
    c. Bend allowance line
    d. Bend tangent line

27. Which of these is true?
    a. An open angle is an angle of less than 90°.
    b. The sum of the mold line dimensions is always greater than the total developed width.
    c. The neutral axis has the same length as the bend tangent line.
    d. The bend allowance equals the sum of the mold line-to-mold point distance times two.

28. What is the minimum bend radius for 7075-T6 aluminum alloy that is 4/5 of an inch thick?
    a. 0.44 inch
    b. 0.38 inch
    c. 0.22 inch
    d. 0.09 inch

29. Say you want to put a 60° bend in a piece of 2024-O aluminum alloy that is 0.050 inch thick. What is the setback?
    a. 0.5773 inch
    b. 0.02887 inch
    c. 0.03464 inch
    d. 0.0635 inch

30. What is the flat line dimension if the mold line dimension is 6 inches if there is one bend and the setback is 0.25 inch?
    a. 6.25 inches
    b. 6 inches
    c. 5.75 inches
    d. 5.50 inches

31. What is the bend allowance for a 90° bend with a radius of 0.2 inch if the material is 0.05 inch thick?
    a. 0.3859 inch
    b. 0.3534 inch
    c. 0.3664 inch
    d. 0.3782 inch

32. Use the bend allowance chart (Figure 4-128) to find the bend allowance for a 90° bend in material 0.04 inch thick with a radius of 3/16 of an inch.
    a. 0.323 inch
    b. 0.003034 inch
    c. 0.077 inch
    d. 0.372 inch

33. Use the J-chart (Figure 4-132) to find the total developed length when the mold line dimensions are 2 inches and 3 inches, the material is 0.075 inch thick, the radius is 0.16 inch, and the angle is 75°.
    a. 5.075 inches
    b. 4.890 inches
    c. 5.110 inches
    d. 4.780 inches

34. This method of forming is difficult because there is no exact forming block to guide the operation.
    a. Block bumping
    b. Sandbag bumping
    c. Forming a concave flange
    d. V-block forming

35. These are cut in rib sections, fuselage frames, and other structural parts to decrease weight—but only where authorized.
    a. Lightening holes
    b. Joggles
    c. Flanges
    d. Stringers

Chapter 4
Aircraft Metal Structural Repair

MULTIPLE CHOICE QUESTIONS

name:

date:

36. Particles of this metal must be kept away from sources of ignition because they burn very easily and can even cause an explosion.
    a. Aluminum
    b. Titanium
    c. Magnesium
    d. Both B and C

37. When performing a sheet metal repair, it is most important to:
    a. Maintain original contour
    b. Minimize weight
    c. Maintain original strength
    d. All of these are equally important

38. These parts are most prone to vibration or flutter if a repair is not performed correctly.
    a. Flight control surfaces
    b. Stringers
    c. Landing gear
    d. Wing tips

39. A small, thin section of metal extending beyond a regular surface, usually at a corner or on the edge of a hole, is called:
    a. A dent
    b. A gall
    c. A burr
    d. An inclusion

40. Damage this type of aircraft skin must usually involve some sort of special fastener instead of solid-shaft rivets.
    a. Closed skin
    b. Open skin
    c. Stressed skin
    d. Nonpressurized skin

Chapter 4
Aircraft Metal Structural Repair

ANALYSIS
QUESTIONS

name:

date:

1. Explain how to drill a hole in sheet metal.

2. What adjustments must be made to a bar folding machine before it can be used correctly?

3. What is the effect of shrinking and stretching on a metal's thickness and workability? Which is more difficult to perform—shrinking or stretching?

Chapter 4
Aircraft Metal Structural Repair

ANALYSIS QUESTIONS

name:

date:

4. What are some reference materials you can use when determining what type of metal to use in a repair?

5. Say a box of rivets bears this code: MS20 426 D 7-9. What does each part of that code tell you about the rivets in the box, and what would you expect to find on the head of each rivet?

6. Describe how to lay out a three-row rivet pattern.

7. What can happen if a countersunk rivet is installed in metal that is too thin for the rivet? What can you do in locations where the metal is too thin for countersinking?

8. Describe how you would lay out the material to form a U-channel piece out of 0.050-inch-thick 5052 aluminum. The legs of the channel are 1 inch high and the flat is 2 inches wide and the bends are 90°.

Chapter 4
Aircraft Metal Structural Repair

ANALYSIS QUESTIONS

name:

date:

Chapter 4
Aircraft Metal Structural Repair

ANALYSIS QUESTIONS

name:

date:

9. Damage to metal parts and structures can be grouped into four general classes. Name them and give a brief description of what is done in each case.

10. What are some considerations a technician must take into account when repairing the leading edge of a wing?

Chapter 5
Aircraft Welding

FILL IN THE BLANK QUESTIONS

name:

date:

1. _____ is accomplished by heating the ends or edges of metal parts to a molten state with a high temperature flame.

2. _____ is the most common type of welding and is usually referred to as "stick" welding.

3. In _____ welding, unlike other types of electric arc welding, the electrode is not consumed; rather, a filler rod is manually fed into the molten puddle.

4. Current flows through the material and the two copper electrodes on a/an _____ machine, and the greater resistance of the material compared to the copper melts the material and forces the molten spots to unite.

5. _____ systems can cut all electrically conductive metals, including aluminum and stainless steel; works well on thin metals; and can successfully cut brass and copper in excess of two inches thick.

6. A welding hose is typically a double hose: the _____ hose is red and has left-hand threads, while the _____ hose is green and has right-hand threads.

7. In oxy-acetylene welding, the size of the _____, not the temperature, determines the amount of heat applied to the work.

8. An acetylene cylinder that has a capacity of 350 cubic feet has a maximum withdrawal of _____ cubic feet per hour.

9. A/An _____ flame is produced by burning more acetylene than oxygen, and it is used for welding high-carbon steel, aluminum, nickel, and Monel.

10. Filler rod is added to the puddle in the amount that provides for the completed fillet to be built up about _____ the thickness of the base metal.

11. When welding _____ that's more than 3/16 inch thick, the surrounding area must be preheated to a temperature between 300 °F and 400 °F before beginning to weld so that a brittle grain structure does not result.

12. Lead, copper, magnesium, and aluminum are classified as _____ metals because they contain no iron.

13. _____ requires less heat than welding and can be used to join metals that can be damaged by high heat, but the strength of the resulting joint is not as great as that of a welded joint.

14. Half-and-half is the most common general-purpose solder, so named because it contains equal portions of _____ and _____.

Chapter 5
Aircraft Welding

FILL IN THE BLANK QUESTIONS

name:

date:

15. _____ is used in brazing and soldering to clean the surface area to be joined and promote flow by capillary action into the joint.

16. When TIG welding aluminum, _____ is preferred as a shielding gas because it provides better cover and better cleaning action than the alternative gas, helium.

17. In TIG welding, the welding _____ is established by touching the base metal plate with the electrode and immediately withdrawing it only about 1/4 inch or less from the base.

18. If the arc is broken during the welding of a bead and the electrode is removed quickly, a/an _____ is formed at the point where the arc ends by the pressure of the gases from the electrode tip forcing the weld metal away from the bead.

19. _____ welds are used to make tee and lap joints.

20. The _____ setting should be lower for welding in the vertical position than for welding in the flat position for similar size electrodes.

21. Uneven heating of metal causes uneven _____, which sets up stresses within the metal.

22. A/An _____ is made by placing two pieces of material edge to edge, without overlap, and then welding.

23. Dents in steel tubing at a/an _____ weld can be repaired by welding a formed steel patch plate over the dented area and surrounding tubes.

24. Assemblies that were originally heat treated must be heat treated again after _____.

25. _____ welds are holes, typically one-fourth the diameter of the original tube, drilled in the outer splice and welded around the circumference for attachment to the inner replacement tube or original tube structure.

Chapter 5
Aircraft Welding

MULTIPLE CHOICE QUESTIONS

name:

date:

1. In shielded metal arc welding (also known as stick welding), the molten puddle of metal is shielded from oxygen by:
    a. Acetylene
    b. Tungsten
    c. Helium
    d. An inert gas released from melted flux

2. This type of welding typically uses a low-voltage, high-current DC power source.
    a. Gas tungsten arc welding
    b. Gas metal arc welding
    c. Shielded metal arc welding
    d. Oxy-acetylene welding

3. In TIG welding, the power supply should be set to AC for:
    a. Butt welds
    b. Welding mild steel or stainless steel
    c. Welding aluminum or magnesium
    d. Welding titanium

4. In plasma arc welding, the plasma gas is usually:
    a. Helium
    b. Acetylene
    c. Nitrogen
    d. Argon

5. This colorless, odorless, and highly flammable gas is used in underwater welding.
    a. Argon
    b. Hydrogen
    c. Helium
    d. Oxygen

6. This important piece of welding gear prevents a high-pressure flame or oxygen-fuel mixture from being pushed back into either cylinder and causing an explosion.
    a. Check valve
    b. Flashback arrestor
    c. Pressure regulator
    d. Equal pressure torch

7. Out of this list of torches, which one uses the highest pressure?
    a. Equal pressure torch
    b. Injector torch
    c. Flaming torch
    d. Cutting torch

8. What can happen if the filler rod is too small in diameter?
    a. It draws heat away from the weld and chills the puddle
    b. Not enough inert gas is released
    c. The heat is not conducted away from the puddle rapidly enough and a burned hole results
    d. The sodium in the flux flares a brilliant yellow-orange

9. If torch tips are operated at less than the required volume of gas:
    a. Starvation
    b. Tip overheating
    c. Possible flashbacks
    d. All of these

10. This type of flame burns at about 6,300 °F.
    a. Neutral
    b. Oxidizing
    c. Carburizing
    d. Cutting

11. Which of these should not be welded with a neutral flame?
    a. Low-carbon steel
    b. Stainless steel
    c. Chrome molybdenum
    d. Aluminum

12. Special attention must be paid when setting up a weld of magnesium, and rigid fixtures should be avoided because of magnesium's:
    a. Low boiling point
    b. Large expansion rate
    c. Small expansion rate
    d. Flammability

Chapter 5
Aircraft Welding

MULTIPLE CHOICE QUESTIONS

name:

date:

13. The principle use of silver solder in aircraft work is:
    a. In the fabrication of high-pressure oxygen lines and other parts that must withstand vibration and high temperatures
    b. Electrical connections
    c. Heat exchanger or radiator cores
    d. Structural repairs

14. The electrode used in TIG welding will start an arc more easily and provide a wider arc shape if it is ground so that it is:
    a. Blunter
    b. Wider
    c. Longer
    d. Sharper

15. A dark blue film on a titanium weld indicates:
    a. That the shielding is satisfactory and the heat affected zone and backup was properly purged until weld temperatures dropped
    b. That the weld must be completely removed and replaced
    c. Slightly contaminated, but unlikely to cause structural deficiency
    d. That the wrong filler material was used

16. In arc welding, if the electrode is moved along the weld too quickly: (
    a. A wide, overlapping bead head forms
    b. The electrode freezes to the plate
    c. The bead is too narrow and there is little or no fusion
    d. The arc makes a sharp cracking sound

17. An arc weld should have the edges beveled and be done in multiple passes on any plate thicker than:
    a. 1/8 inch
    b. 1/4 inch
    c. 5/8 inch
    d. 1/2 inch

18. Butt joints where the metal to be welded is 1/4-inch thick or more should be welded with a:
    a. Fillet weld
    b. Bead weld
    c. Groove weld
    d. Lap weld

19. Welding a seam more than 10 to 12 inches long tends to:
    a. Push the edges of the plates apart as the weld progresses
    b. Cause increased splatter and slag
    c. Draw the seam together as the weld progresses
    d. Require more flux than would otherwise be used

20. A gas weld should have the edges beveled on any plate thicker than:
    a. 1/8 inch
    b. 1/4 inch
    c. 5/8 inch
    d. 1/2 inch

Chapter 5
Aircraft Welding

ANALYSIS QUESTIONS

name:

date:

1. Compare the equipment used in gas welding and stick welding.

2. Explain the function of the inert gas in gas metal arc welding and gas tungsten arc welding.

3. Describe the characteristics of a well-executed gas weld.

4. Describe the characteristics of a well-executed stick weld on a flat plate.

Chapter 5
Aircraft Welding

ANALYSIS QUESTIONS

name:

date:

5. What methods can be used to control expansion and contraction when performing a straight butt weld to join two sheets?

Chapter 6
Aircraft Wood and Structural Repair

FILL IN THE BLANK QUESTIONS

name:

date:

1. The largest wooden aircraft ever constructed was the _____, which had an empty weight of 300,000 pounds and was powered by eight radial engines, each producing 3,000 horsepower.

2. Before inspecting an aircraft constructed of wood components, check the moisture in the structure using a meter; the ideal moisture range is _____ percent.

3. When inspecting a glued joint, any penetration observed through the use of a/an _____ means that the joint is defective.

4. Dark discolorations of the wood or gray stains running along the grain indicate _____, and if it can't be removed by light scraping, you must replace the part.

5. To detect _____ failures in wooden structural members, shine a flashlight beam along the member parallel to the grain and look for minute ridges running across the grain.

6. In all types of aircraft wood, the slope of the grain cannot be steeper than _____.

7. _____ glue and _____ glue both deteriorate under moisture and thermal variation, but resorcinol glue has good wet-weather and UV resistance and is therefore a better choice.

8. The period between the application of the adhesive and putting the parts of the joint together is called the _____ time.

9. Adhesive _____ is the time elapsed from the mixing of the adhesive components until the mixture must be discarded, because it no longer performs to its specifications.

10. All gluing operations should be performed when the ambient temperature is above _____ °F for proper performance of the adhesive.

11. A/An _____ joint is the most satisfactory method of fabricating an end joint between two solid wood members.

12. Doublers used to repair a longitudinal crack in a spar must extend beyond the ends of the crack at least _____ times the width of the spar, and the ends should be feathered out to a 5:1 slope.

13. For boring accurate and smooth holes in a wood structure, a/an _____ should be used whenever possible.

Chapter 6
Aircraft Wood and Structural Repair

FILL IN THE BLANK QUESTIONS

name:

date:

14. A/An _____ can generally be used on repair holes in plywood aircraft skin, if the hole is not more than 1 inch in diameter.

15. A/An _____ patch, the best repair for damaged plywood, has edges beveled at a 12:1 slope, but a/an _____ patch's edges are beveled at a 5:1 slope.

Chapter 6
Aircraft Wood and Structural Repair

MULTIPLE CHOICE QUESTIONS

name:

date:

1. Most airplanes were constructed of wood frames with fabric coverings during:
   a. World War I
   b. World War II
   c. The 1950s
   d. The 1960s

2. Title 14 of the *Code of Federal Regulations* Part 65 states that a certificated mechanic may not perform any work for which he or she is rated unless:
   a. He or she has performed the work concerned at an earlier date
   b. He or she lacks prior experience, but is supervised by an appropriately rated person who has that experience
   c. He or she has worked in the current position for more than five years
   d. Both A and B

3. Some aircraft parts are made of this type of wood, which is an assembled product of wood and glue made up of an odd number of veneers laid up with the grain of each layer placed 90° to the adjacent layer.
   a. Solid wood
   b. Laminated wood
   c. Plywood
   d. Compreg

4. The preferred choice for aircraft wood, and the standard to which all other wood is compared, is:
   a. Oak
   b. Spruce
   c. Douglas fir
   d. Yellow poplar

5. All of these wood types can be used as a direct substitute for spruce in the same sizes except:
   a. Douglas fir
   b. Northern white pine
   c. Port Orford white cedar
   d. Western hemlock

6. Mineral streaks are acceptable in replacement wood unless:
   a. Closer inspection reveals decay
   b. The streaks are more than 10 inches long
   c. They are not along the edges of rectangular beams
   d. They are less than 20 inches from other mineral streaks

7. This is a clamping device with two rigid wood bars used to keep an assembly of flat panel boards aligned during glue-up.
   a. Adhesive
   b. Form
   c. Caul
   d. Glue line

8. When applying force to a glued joint, maximum strength will be obtained if:
   a. The force is concentrated in two spots at either end of the work
   b. The force is greater than 200 psi
   c. The force is applied immediately after the parts are joined
   d. The force is applied evenly

9. This is a flat piece of plywood used to reinforce splice repairs.
   a. Scarf
   b. Gusset
   c. Stringer
   d. Cap strip

10. Plywood skin may be repaired with this type of patch if the skin is not more than 1/10-inch thick and the largest dimension of the hole to be repaired is no more than 15 times the skin thickness.
    a. Overlay patch
    b. Surface patch
    c. Plug patch
    d. Splayed patch

Chapter 6
Aircraft Wood and Structural Repair

ANALYSIS QUESTIONS

name:

date:

1. What developments led to the decline of wood structures in aircraft construction?

2. What can cause the premature deterioration of a glue joint?

3. Name some signs of wood decay and dry rot.

Chapter 6
Aircraft Wood and Structural Repair

ANALYSIS QUESTIONS

name:

date:

4. Describe how you can cut an accurate scarf.

5. How can you tell whether a bolt or bushing hole in a wooden aircraft structural part is acceptable? What can happen if it is not?

Chapter 7
Advanced Composite Materials

FILL IN THE BLANK QUESTIONS

name:

date:

1. A/An _____ material like aluminum or titanium has uniform properties in all directions.

2. A/An _____ material, where a fiber is the primary load-carrying element, is only strong and stiff in the direction of the fibers.

3. The strength and stiffness of a composite buildup depends on the _____ of the plies.

4. A/An _____ is a single grouping of filament or fiber ends, with all filaments not twisted and running in the same direction.

5. The advantages of carbon fiber include high strength and _____ resistance.

6. When the components of the resin have been mixed but the chemical reaction has not started, the resin is in the _____ and you can perform the wet layup procedure.

7. _____ material consists of a combination of a matrix and a fiber reinforcement, and it must be stored in a freezer to retard the curing process.

8. _____ materials, such as carbon, glass, and Kevlar, are impregnated with a resin just before the repair work starts and can therefore be stored at room temperature for a long period.

9. _____ construction consists of two relatively thin sheets of facing material bonded to and separated by a relatively thick, lightweight core.

10. Delamination, resin-rich areas, and wrinkles in composite materials are considered _____ defects.

11. Audio or sonic testing is a surprisingly accurate (when performed by experienced personnel) means of detecting delamination and disbond in composite materials; it's more commonly known as _____ testing.

12. _____ ultrasonic inspection uses two transducers, one on each side of the area to be inspected, and measures the loss of an ultrasonic signal from one to the other.

13. The aluminum _____ that supports a wet layup part during the cure cycle is covered with a parting film so that the part doesn't stick to it.

14. _____ material provides a path for air to get out of the vacuum bag, and _____ material creates a path for air and volatiles to escape from the repair.

Chapter 7
Advanced Composite Materials

FILL IN THE BLANK QUESTIONS

name:

date:

15. A/An _____ is a thermoelectric device used to accurately measure temperatures and is composed of a wire with two leads of dissimilar metals joined at one end and connected to a monitor.

16. During the _____ process, a dry fabric is impregnated with a resin that is mixed just before making the repair.

17. _____ is a process frequently used for removable aircraft parts in which the part to be repaired is completely enclosed in a vacuum bag or the bag is wrapped around the end of the component to obtain an adequate seal.

18. All prepreg materials, as well as some wet layup repairs, are cured with a/an _____ cure cycle.

19. A potted repair can be used to repair damage to a sandwich honeycomb structure if the damage is smaller than _____ inch, but this will not restore the full strength of the part.

20. The _____ in a repair must be oriented in the same direction as the original layers.

21. _____ repairs involve drilling two holes on the outside of a delamination area in a lightly loaded solid laminate.

22. Aircraft _____, which are electronic windows for the radar, are often made of nonconducting honeycomb sandwich structure with only three or four plies of fiberglass.

23. The _____ method improves the quality of a wet layup repair by removing the entrapped air that can cause porosity in a regular wet layup, and is often used to make patches for solid laminate structures with complexly contoured surfaces.

24. _____ repairs are quicker and easier to fabricate than bonded repairs, but they are prohibited in honeycomb sandwich assemblies because of the potential for moisture intrusion and the core degradation that would follow.

25. _____ and _____ fasteners corrode if used with carbon fiber.

26. A fastener made of a/an _____ alloy is most commonly used with carbon fiber reinforced composites.

Chapter 7
Advanced Composite Materials

FILL IN THE BLANK QUESTIONS

name:

date:

27. _____ used for carbon fiber and fiberglass are made from diamond-coated material or solid carbide because the fibers are so hard that standard types do not last long.

28. The general rule for cutting composites is _____ speed and _____ feed.

29. The acrylic plastic commonly used for windows and canopies can be softened by heat and is therefore considered a/an _____ material.

30. A/An _____ cement is a cement to which a catalyst is added to promote rapid hardening, and this type of cement is suitable for all types of Plexiglas acrylic cast sheet and parts molded from Plexiglas pellets.

Chapter 7
Advanced Composite Materials

MULTIPLE CHOICE QUESTIONS

name:

date:

1. Structural properties of composite laminates, such as stiffness, dimensional stability, and strength, depend on:
   a. The number of plies
   b. The shape of the materials used
   c. The stacking sequence and orientation of the plies
   d. The resin that holds the plies together

2. A diagram or spec sheet uses this to describe the direction of fibers.
   a. Warp clock
   b. Fiber form
   c. Strand yarn
   d. Yarn tow

3. This manufactured fiber is known for its high resistance to impact damage, but it is prone to water absorption.
   a. Fiberglass
   b. Aramid (Kevlar)
   c. Carbon
   d. Ceramic fiber

4. The surface of an external composite component often includes a layer of conductive material to protect the aircraft structures from:
   a. Water damage
   b. Delamination
   c. Cracking
   d. Lightning strikes

5. This type of matrix material is often used for interior components because of its low smoke and flammability characteristics.
   a. Polyimides
   b. Phenolic resin
   c. Epoxy
   d. Vinyl ester resin

6. This matrix material requires the highest cure temperature.
   a. Polyimides
   b. Phenolic resin
   c. Epoxy
   d. Vinyl ester resin

7. Fully cured resin is said to be in:
   a. Stage A
   b. Stage B
   c. Stage C
   d. Stage D

8. The cells of this style of honeycomb material are rectangular.
   a. Bisected
   b. Flexicore
   c. Overexpanded
   d. Polystyrene

9. Thermal inspection of composite structures works because:
   a. Defects conduct heat more efficiently than defect-free areas.
   b. Defect-free areas conduct heat more efficiently than areas with defects.
   c. Flaws can be detected parallel to the direction of the heat source.
   d. Moisture when heated tends to boil, and the steam generated shows the location of defects.

10. These thin layers are used to create a clean surface for bonding purposes.
    a. Bleeder ply
    b. Layup tape
    c. Release film
    d. Peel ply

11. This material is used to protect a heat blanket or caul plate from resin that would otherwise bleed through.
    a. Solid release film
    b. Vacuum bag
    c. Layup tape
    d. Peel ply

Chapter 7
Advanced Composite Materials

MULTIPLE CHOICE QUESTIONS

name:

date:

12. Which of these is bad advice regarding the placement of thermocouples?
    a. Never use fewer than three thermocouples to monitor a heating cycle.
    b. Place at least one thermocouple under the vacuum port.
    c. Place flash tape above and below the thermocouple tips to protect them from resin flash.
    d. Thermocouples around the perimeter of the repair patch should be about 0.5 inch from the edge of the adhesive line.

13. Trapped air is removed from a multi-layered prepreg part through a process called:
    a. Autoclaving
    b. Adhesion
    c. Stacking
    d. Consolidation

14. Prepreg systems with 32 to 35 percent resin content are typically considered:
    a. No-bleed systems
    b. Controlled bleed systems
    c. Edge bleedout systems
    d. Precured

15. An elevated temperature cure cycle consists of what segments in which order?
    a. Precure, cool, soak
    b. Ramp up, hold, cool down
    c. Layup, prepreg, form
    d. Form, hold, bleed

16. After you make a repair to a composite flight control surface, you must:
    a. Check the repair in a wind tunnel
    b. Perform a lateral check
    c. Perform a balance check
    d. Use a plumb bob to check aircraft alignment

17. One of the drawbacks of performing this type of repair on a solid laminate structure is that the taper angle requires a considerable amount of sound material to be removed from the repair site.
    a. Bolted repair
    b. Scarved or tapered repair
    c. Co-bonded repair
    d. A repair involving Kevlar

18. Boron epoxy, GLARE, and graphite epoxy are composite materials that can be used to inhibit crack growth and provide an alternate load path around the crack in:
    a. Aluminum, steel, and titanium components
    b. Honeycomb-core components
    c. Solid laminate components
    d. None of these

19. If a composite panel must be removed periodically for maintenance, this type of fastener is recommended:
    a. Screws and nutplates
    b. Fiberlite
    c. Blind bolts such as the Cherry Maxibolt
    d. Hi-Lok fasteners

20. Which of these materials is suitable for cleaning the transparent plastics used on aircraft?
    a. Alcohol
    b. Acetone
    c. Water and mild soap
    d. All of these

Chapter 7
Advanced Composite Materials

ANALYSIS QUESTIONS

name:

date:

1. Explain how the orientation of the fibers in a composite buildup provides strength and stiffness to the structure.

2. What is the function of matrix material, and what are three common types of matrix material?

3. Define prepreg materials. What is the opposite of prepreg material? What are the advantages and disadvantages of each?

Chapter 7
Advanced Composite Materials

ANALYSIS QUESTIONS

name:

date:

4. What happens if a part has too little resin? What happens if it has too much? What is the ideal fiber-to-resin ratio?

5. Say you suspect water has gotten into a composite structure. What are three ways to test for that defect without destroying the structure? Briefly describe how each one works.

Chapter 8
Aircraft Painting and Finishing

FILL IN THE BLANK QUESTIONS

name:

date:

1. A highly flammable solvent used in paints, surface coatings, and in paint remover, _____ is also used in high-solids coatings to reduce emissions because it evaporates quickly.

2. _____, also known as white spirit, Stoddard solvent, or petroleum spirit, is the most widely used solvent in the paint industry.

3. Made from flax seeds, _____ is commonly used as a carrier in oil paint—it makes paint more fluid, transparent, and glossy.

4. A/An _____ is the foundation of a finish—it bonds to the surface, inhibits metal corrosion, and provides an anchor for the finish coats.

5. The most common finishing coat in aviation use today is _____, which provides excellent resistance to abrasions, stains, chemicals, and UV rays.

6. The air supply for paint spraying comes from an air compressor with a storage tank that can provide no less than _____ psi and _____ CFM of air to the gun.

7. Anyone who is spraying coatings that contain isocyanides or chromate primers must wear a/an _____.

8. Paint _____ can be measured with a Zahn cup.

9. Primer is typically applied using a/an _____ spray pattern in which alternating passes of the spray gun are perpendicular to one another.

10. _____ is a dull, milky haze that appears in a paint finish, the result of moisture being trapped in the paint.

11. _____ are small holes in the coating and are almost always due to the surface not being cleaned of all traces of silicone wax.

12. An incorrect setting on the spray guy can result in _____, meaning that the atomized spray particles dry before reaching the surface being painted.

13. The preferred masking materials for trim lines are _____ tape and quality masking paper.

14. The first character in the identification marking of an aircraft with a U.S. registration is _____.

15. While some older chemical paint stripping products are harmful to the environment or people, _____ eliminates these concerns because it removes paint and primer coats with soft, angular particles that can be reused.

Chapter 8
Aircraft Painting and Finishing

MULTIPLE CHOICE QUESTIONS

name:

date:

1. Which of these solvents can be used to clean paint equipment and brushes that have been used with oil-based paints?
   a. Turpentine
   b. Methyl chloride
   c. Acetone
   d. Toluene

2. This two-part primer requires a chemical activator to cure, but it is easy to sand and fills well when applied over a wash primer.
   a. Gray enamel
   b. Dope
   c. Epoxy
   d. Urethane

3. Older types of this paint tended to yellow with age, but newer versions—though easy to apply—are susceptible to damage from bird droppings, acid rain, and gasoline spills.
   a. Dope
   b. Lacquer
   c. Synthetic enamel
   d. Polyurethane

4. When applied by spray gun, primers do not tend to run because:
   a. Of their chemical properties
   b. They are applied in light coats.
   c. The spray gun is moved more quickly than with paint.
   d. Primers are sprayed at higher pressure than paint.

5. Any of these conditions can cause poor paint adhesion with the exception of:
   a. Application of the wrong primer
   b. Improper thinning of the coating material
   c. Wrong size spray nozzle
   d. Improper surface preparation

6. This bumpy paint surface condition can be caused by using insufficient reducer, material that was not uniformly mixed, or forced drying with fans or heat that is done too quickly.
   a. Orange peel
   b. Pinholes
   c. Sags
   d. Wrinkling

7. Rapid changes in the air temperature during spraying, excessively thick coating, or applying a second heavy coat before the first one dries can result in this condition, which requires the complete removal of the paint.
   a. Orange peel
   b. Pinholes
   c. Sags
   d. Wrinkling

8. Before decals are applied, the surface should be cleaned with:
   a. Soap and water
   b. Plastic media blasting
   c. Aliphatic naphtha
   d. Benzene

9. If you wipe a painted surface with a rag dampened by MEK and it comes away with pigment from the paint:
   a. Repeat the test using turbine engine oil
   b. The surface is probably an acrylic finish
   c. The surface is probably an epoxy finish
   d. You must sand the surface and recoat

10. The most significant hazards for technicians involved in painting, stripping, or refinishing aircraft involve:
    a. Airborne chemicals that can be inhaled
    b. Skin irritation
    c. Fire
    d. None of these

Chapter 8
Aircraft Painting and Finishing

ANALYSIS QUESTIONS

name:

date:

1. The term "paint" encompasses several different products. Name them, and describe the purpose of paint on an aircraft.

2. Describe how to prepare a bare aluminum surface for painting.

3. How do you properly adjust a spray gun?

Chapter 8
Aircraft Painting and Finishing

ANALYSIS QUESTIONS

name:

date:

4. How should paint be applied using a spray gun?

5. When and with what equipment should you protect yourself during the painting and refinishing process?

Chapter 9
Aircraft Electrical System

FILL IN THE BLANK QUESTIONS

name:

date:

1. Ohm's law states that the current through a conductor is directly proportional to the _____ and inversely proportional to the _____.

2. In a light where the resistance is 4 Ω and the current is 3 A, the voltage is _____.

3. Electrical current is the movement of free _____.

4. The push or pressure from one end of a conductor to the other is known as _____ or _____.

5. The resistance of a metallic conductor is directly proportional to its _____.

6. Electromagnetic _____ is the process of producing a voltage by moving a magnetic field in relation to a conductor.

7. The _____ voltage of an AC circuit is 0.707 times the peak value, and it is the one most commonly displayed on an AC meter.

8. The _____ is the number of AC cycles per second.

9. When two signals reach their peak value at the same time and reach zero at the same time, the two sine waves are said to be _____.

10. The induced voltage that opposes the applied voltage is called _____, and is also known as the counter EMF.

11. Capacitance, usually measured in _____, is the capability of a body to hold an electric charge.

12. The total opposition to current flow in an AC circuit is known as _____ and is represented by the letter _____.

13. AC circuits have two types of power: _____ power, which is the power consumed by the resistance portion of the circuit; and _____ power, which is the power consumed by the entire circuit, including the resistance and reactance.

14. _____ must be added to a dry-charged lead-acid battery when it is placed into service and then periodically replenished.

15. The capacity of a battery is measured in _____ delivered at a specified discharge rate to a cut-off voltage, usually 1 V per cell.

16. In most aircraft, the battery charging system is of the constant _____ type, and involves an engine-driven generator connected through the aircraft electrical system directly to the battery.

Chapter 9
Aircraft Electrical System

FILL IN THE BLANK QUESTIONS

name:

date:

17. The rotating portion of a DC generator is called the _____, and it produces an AC voltage that is changed to DC voltage by a _____.

18. DC generators can have _____ windings, compound windings, or _____ windings, but the latter type is never used in aircraft because of its poor voltage and current regulation.

19. High-output generators have the advantage of combining two units in one housing: they generate electrical power and also _____ the engine.

20. The three field windings in a typical DC alternator produce a three-phase AC voltage that is converted to DC by a/an _____ assembly.

21. A/An _____ is a device that converts DC power into AC power.

22. An aircraft AC alternator must rotate at about 400 Hz for the electrical system to operate properly, so a/an _____ is used to ensure that the alternator rotates at the correct speed.

23. A/An _____ is an electrical fault that occurs when a circuit creates an unwanted connection.

24. Because starter motors can draw 100 A or more, they are controlled through a/an _____.

25. The process of equalizing the outputs of the two alternators or generators on a twin-engine aircraft is often called _____.

26. A hot _____ is directly connected to the aircraft battery, and thus is always able to provide power for basic items like entry door lighting and a clock.

27. In a typical large aircraft, the generator control unit (GCU) controls AC generator functions and the _____ is used to control the distribution of electrical power throughout the aircraft.

28. The standard wire in light aircraft is MIL-W-5086A, which uses a tin-coated copper conductor rated at _____ V and temperatures of 105 °C.

29. Insulation resistance is the resistance of a material to _____ leakage through and over the surface of the material.

30. _____ is the process of applying a metallic covering to wiring to eliminate electromagnetic interference (EMI).

Chapter 9
Aircraft Electrical System

FILL IN THE BLANK QUESTIONS

name:

date:

31. Wire bundles should generally include fewer than _____ wires, or be no more than 1 1/2 to 2 inches in diameter, when practicable.

32. The radius of a bend in a wire bundle must be more than _____ the diameter of the largest wire or cable in the bundle.

33. Clamps on wire bundles should be tight enough that they do not allow the bundle to move through the clamp when a slight pull is applied; however, clamps on _____ cables should allow the cable to move slightly when tugged.

34. _____ means that conductive objects are electrically connected in such a way that either a conductive structure or some other return path is provided to allow the safe completion of a normal or fault circuit.

35. Before wire can be connected to terminals or splices, the _____ must be stripped from the connecting ends to expose the bare conductor.

36. A/An _____ is used to collect, organize, and distribute circuits to the appropriate harnesses that are attached to the equipment and to house components such as relays and diodes.

37. A/An _____-pole _____-throw switch turns two circuits on and off with one lever.

38. A/An _____ consists of a strip of metal enclosed in a glass or plastic housing; it is installed in series with the voltage source, and if the current exceeds capacity, the metal strip breaks.

39. A set of FAA-mandated _____ lights consists of one red light, one green light, and one white light; the _____ light is always mounted on the tip of the right wing.

40. The most powerful lights on the exterior of an aircraft are usually the _____ lights, used to illuminate the runway at night.

Chapter 9
Aircraft Electrical System

MULTIPLE CHOICE QUESTIONS

name:

date:

1. Which of these is *not* a valid statement of Ohm's law?
   a. E = I x R
   b. R = E / I
   c. I = E / R
   d. R = I / E

2. Current can be measured in:
   a. Amps
   b. Volts
   c. Ohms
   d. Henrys

3. According to electron theory:
   a. Electrons flow from out of a positive source into an area that lacks charge.
   b. Electrons flow from an abundance of electrons in a negative source toward an area that lacks electrons.
   c. The pressure of electron flow is the result of relatively high resistance from a conductor.
   d. Resistance and current vary directly.

4. If the voltage at one point in the circuit is 16 V and at another point, the voltage is 13.4 V, then 2.6 V is the:
   a. EMF
   b. Applied voltage
   c. Voltage drop
   d. Direct voltage

5. Materials like rubber, glass, and ceramics are considered:
   a. Conductors
   b. Resistors
   c. Reactors
   d. Insulators

6. A primary battery produces electricity by what means?
   a. Chemical reaction
   b. Piezoelectric effect
   c. Photovoltaic action
   d. Induction

7. The relative motion between a conductor and a magnetic field produces:
   a. An EMF in the conductor
   b. Current, if the conductor is part of a complete circuit
   c. Magnetism
   d. Both A and B

8. Which of these would *not* increase the voltage and current generated via electromagnetic induction?
   a. Adding more loops to the conductor coil
   b. Using a stronger electromagnet
   c. Reversing the polarity of the magnet
   d. Making the conductor rotate faster

9. The voltage at a certain time in the AC cycle is called:
   a. Peak voltage
   b. Effective voltage
   c. Alternating voltage
   d. Instantaneous voltage

10. The frequency of an AC cycle is measured in:
    a. Milliseconds
    b. Hz
    c. CPS
    d. Both B and C

11. The time required for a sine wave to complete one full cycle is called:
    a. The period
    b. The wavelength
    c. The frequency
    d. The waveform

12. The counter EMF that opposes any change in current through a coil is called:
    a. Resistance
    b. Inductance
    c. Capacitance
    d. Insulation

Chapter 9
Aircraft Electrical System

MULTIPLE CHOICE QUESTIONS

name:

date:

13. Say a circuit has four inductances connected in parallel, and each inductance is measured at 10 Ω. What is the total reactance?
    a. 40 Ω
    b. 20 Ω
    c. 5 Ω
    d. 2.5 Ω

14. Impedance is represented by the symbol:
    a. Z
    b. π
    c. X_C
    d. X_L

15. What is the true power in a circuit with 8 A of current and 3 Ω resistance?
    a. 24 watts
    b. 83 watts
    c. 192 watts
    d. 576 watts

16. If the true power in a circuit is 150 watts and the apparent power is 200 volt-amps, what is the power factor?
    a. 350
    b. 75
    c. 133
    d. 90

17. The specific gravity of the electrolyte is an indication of the state of charge in what types of batteries?
    a. Lead-acid
    b. Nickel-cadmium
    c. Neither of these
    d. Both A and B

18. In a DC generator, what part consists of windings wound around an iron core and the commutator?
    a. The field coil
    b. The field frame
    c. The inverter
    d. The armature

19. Which of these statements regarding aircraft batteries and DC generators is true?
    a. An aircraft's batteries and DC generator should have the same voltage output.
    b. An aircraft's batteries must have a slightly higher voltage output than its DC generator.
    c. An aircraft's DC generator must have a slightly higher voltage output than its batteries.
    d. Each aircraft electrical system is different and it is impossible to generalize.

20. A solid-state generator control unit (GCU) almost always uses this unit to monitor system voltage and control field current and generator output.
    a. Zener diode
    b. Capacitor
    c. Shunt winding
    d. Fuse

21. In a DC alternator, this part receives current from the aircraft battery to produce an electromagnet.
    a. Rectifier
    b. Field winding
    c. Armature
    d. Slip rings

22. On which of these aircraft would you be likely to find an AC alternator?
    a. Light aircraft
    b. Helicopter
    c. Large transport-category aircraft
    d. Ultralight

23. In a brushless alternator, energy from the rotor is transferred via:
    a. Slip rings
    b. Armature
    c. Commutator
    d. Magnetic flux energy

24. AC alternator control units must regulate:
    a. Voltage and current
    b. Voltage and frequency
    c. Current and resistance
    d. Resistance and frequency

Chapter 9
Aircraft Electrical System

MULTIPLE CHOICE QUESTIONS

name:

date:

25. An ammeter connected to the battery circuit will give a positive indication when:
    a. Current is flowing from the main bus to the battery.
    b. Current is leaving the battery.
    c. The master solenoid is switched on.
    d. There are no shorts in the circuit.

26. To monitor the position of each landing gear during operation, these spring-loaded momentary contract items are used:
    a. Avionics buses
    b. Squat swithes
    c. Limit switches
    d. Safety switches

27. The AC generators on a transport category aircraft typically produce:
    a. Three-phase 115-volt AC at 400 Hz
    b. Three-phase 120-volt AC at 470 Hz
    c. Three-phase 110-volt AC at 360 Hz
    d. Four-phase 115-volt AC at 400 Hz

28. This type of wiring diagram illustrates the principle of operation, but does not show parts as they actually appear or function.
    a. Pictorial
    b. Block
    c. Schematic
    d. Exploded panel

29. Which of these is an acceptable definition of a wire, as used in aircraft?
    a. A single, solid conductor covered with an insulating material
    b. A stranded conductor covered with an insulating material
    c. Two or more separately insulated conductors in the same jacket
    d. Both A and B, but not C

30. Two or more separately insulated conductors twisted together, or a single insulated center conductor with a metallic braided outer conductor may be referred to as:
    a. Wires
    b. Cables
    c. Conductors
    d. Wire harnesses

31. Which of these is *not* an advantage of copper wiring over aluminum wiring?
    a. Higher conductivity
    b. Lighter
    c. Greater tensile strength
    d. More ductility

32. Which gauge of wire has a resistance of approximately 1 Ω per 1,000 feet at 77 °F (25 °C)?
    a. #1
    b. #9
    c. #10
    d. #18

33. Identification marking should be placed at each end of a wire and:
    a. At intervals of no more than 10 inches along the length of the wire
    b. Again 12 inches from each end of the wire
    c. Every 6 inches along the length of the wire
    d. At intervals of no more than 15 inches along the length of the wire

34. Whenever possible, wiring should be routed at least how far away from lines carrying oxygen, oil, fuel, hydraulic fluid, or alcohol?
    a. 2 inches
    b. 6 inches
    c. 10 inches
    d. 1 foot

35. This metallic or nonmetallic mechanical protection for cables or wires should have an inner diameter about 25 percent larger than that of the wire bundle.
    a. Clamp
    b. Conduit
    c. Cover
    d. Shielding

Chapter 9
Aircraft Electrical System

MULTIPLE CHOICE QUESTIONS

name:

date:

36. When should wire shielding be used?
    a. In areas of high moisture
    b. In areas of high heat
    c. When the circuit can be affected by crosstalk from another circuit in the harness or bundle
    d. When the bundle or harness passes through a metallic bulkhead

37. The electrical connection of two or more conducting objects not otherwise connected—for example, exterior aircraft parts, or electronic equipment—is called:
    a. Grounding
    b. Bonding
    c. Static conductivity
    d. Lightning prevention

38. Ties or lacing must be used instead of straps to secure wire groups and bundles in these areas:
    a. SWAMP areas
    b. High-vibration areas
    c. Where a strap could be exposed to UV light
    d. All of these

39. Wires are usually joined at a:
    a. Terminal lug
    b. Terminal strip
    c. Terminal connection
    d. Terminal bus

40. Which of these types of switches routes current to one path or to another, such that only one circuit is ON at any time?
    a. Double-pole single-throw
    b. Spring loaded
    c. Double-pole double-throw
    d. Single-pole double-throw

Chapter 9
Aircraft Electrical System

ANALYSIS QUESTIONS

name:

date:

1. Compare conventional current theory and the electron theory description of how electrons move through a conductor. Which is the scientifically accepted version now? Which can be used in troubleshooting circuits?

2. Describe the relationship between current, electromotive force, and resistance.

3. What are some advantages of alternating current over direct current in aircraft usage?

Chapter 9
Aircraft Electrical System

ANALYSIS QUESTIONS

name:

date:

4. Calculate to the nearest ohm the inductive reactance and the capacitive reactance in a 110-volt circuit with a frequency of 50 Hz, an inductance of 0.15 H, and a condenser with a capacitance of 90 mf. If the resistance in the circuit is 10 Ω, what is the impedance? What is the total current, to the nearest tenth of an amp?

5. Compare the construction, maintenance, and performance of lead-acid batteries with nickel-cadmium batteries.

6. Both AC and DC generators have a loop that rotates relative to a magnetic field to generate current. What makes the output of the AC generator an alternating current, and why is the output of a DC generator direct current?

7. What are the components and function of a typical battery circuit on a small single-engine aircraft?

8. What is a SWAMP area, and what precautions do you need to take with wires in such an area?

Chapter 9
Aircraft Electrical System

ANALYSIS QUESTIONS

name:

date:

Chapter 9
Aircraft Electrical System

ANALYSIS QUESTIONS

name:

date:

9. Find the actual circuit content for each wire in this bundle and for the entire bundle: an open harness consisting of 20 #10 copper wires rated at 250 °C and operated in ambient temperatures of 20 °C at sea level and 60 °C at an altitude of 25,000 feet, with all wires operating at or near their maximum capacity.

10. What is the differences between a terminal lug and a connector?